Nyhart Family History

George Washington
"Wash" Nyhart, ca. 1900

Evelyn Nyhart Dodd

Dedication

This publication is dedicated to my children, cousins, and their families. Their belief in me has encouraged me to take on this detective work and writing project. Family is the heart of everything. We are blessed beyond measure with this family.

Preface

The Nyhart family history is nothing short of remarkable. My father, over the years, stressed how important it is to pass down the family history. As my cousins and I talked about times gone by, I decided to memorialize these stories for posterity. I could have traced more generations, yet I focused on the path to Montana and the stories of my early childhood memories. More stories are expected and forthcoming, and I offer these writings to capture the remarkable lives and history that compose our family.

Nyhart Coat of Arms

Introduction

There are at least 30 spellings of the surname Nyhart, which include, Knauwert, Knauert, Nauert, Newert, Neuhert, Neuhardt, Nauharth, Neuthard, Neuhard, Newhard, Newhart, Newhardt, Neihart, Neithart, Neihardt, Neidhart, Neidhard, Neihard, Neyhardt, Neytharrd, Neythart, Neyhart, Neyhard, Nyhard, Nyhart, Nyhardt, Neuthert, Nihart, Nihardt, and Nihard.

The Nyhart genealogy traces back to Conrad Neuhardt, born in 1113. He was born and died in Zweibricken, Germany. He was married to Martha Buck and had two children. Conrad worked as a blacksmith. There was a demand for armor in those days with all the conflicts in Europe and the British Isles. Some of the families were armorers. Conrad became so efficient as an armorer that the German Emperor Fredric Barbarossa elevated Conrad to the dignity of a Patrician, a titled aristocrat. He gave Conrad a coat of arms.

Conrad Coat of Arms

Most Nyharts were farmers, blacksmiths, castle tenders and even mayors. Most were Catholic until 1517 when Monk Martin Luther (the religious reformer) started Lutheranism. At that time, many of the family joined the Protestant faith.

The Nyhart Family

Generation	Period	Family Tree
1	1113 - 1191	Conrad Neuhardt.
2	1165 - 1236	Caspar Neuhart. He married Johanna Bierer and had one child.
3	1205 - 1280	George Neuhart. He married Martha Dauer and had three children.
4	1245- 1317	Andrew Neuhart. He married Anna Frank, and they had one child.

There are five generations with unknown first names, and the dates are approximate.

Generation	Period	Family Tree
5	ca. 1285	Neuhart.
6	ca. 1320	Neuhart.
7	ca. 1355	Neuhart.
8	ca. 1380	Neuhart.
9	ca. 1420	Neuhart.

Generation	Period	Family Tree
10	1460-1512	George Schifferstadt Nauwert. He was a blacksmith. He married Mary Dauer, and they had two children.
11	1490-1560	Hans Andreas Nauert. He married Anna Maria Frank, and they had one child.
12	1518-1589	Johann Friedrich Nauert. He married (unknown name) and had three children.
13	1548-1608	Hans Johannes Nauert. He married Barbara Schartenberger and had two children.
14	1574-1636	Valentine Nauert. He was a farmer and drove ox carts from the ore mine to the smelter. He married Barbara Wagner, and they had five children.

Generation	Period	Family Tree
15	1599-1654	Christophel Neuhart. All known Neuharts descend from a single patriarch, Christophel. He married Margaret Ostertag, and they had eight children. Through our Grandmother Margaret, the Neuharts trace descent from the pharaohs dating back to 1600 B.C. at the time of the XVth Dynasty. Cleopatra was not a direct ancestor but a cousin to the family. The Ostertags family owned many castles.
16	1629-1685	Nicholas Neuhart. He married Anna Catherine Schneider and had eight children during The Thirty-Year War between 1618 and 1648. There was lots of devastation in the area. Years 1635 and 1636 saw the deadly siege of the Bubonic Plague that wiped out much of Europe's population.

Generation	Period	Family Tree
17	1661-1723	Hans Christophel Neuhart. He was an innkeeper in Zweibruecken, Germany. He married Susanna Maria Ringli and had many (unknown count of) children.
18	1716-1800	Johan "George" Neuhart. He was born in Rumbach, Germany and was the first family member to leave Germany for the Americas. He married Anna Catherine Sensinger, and they had nine children.
19	1749-1830	George Neuhart, Jr.. He married Mary Magdalena Sterner and had six children.
20	1774-1821	John Neihart. He married Maria Magdalena Henry, and they had 13 children.

Generation	Period	Family Tree
21	1805-1902	Adam Neihart. His first wife was Susanna Rumbeck, his second wife was Catherine Smith, and his third wife was Ann Parmer. He had nine children with Susanna and one child with Catherine. Adam's third marriage was short and ended in divorce from Ann.
22	1836-1912	George Washington "Wash" Nyhart. He married Mary Linder.
23	1863-1945	Jordan "Jerd" Luccins Nyhart. He married Frances Amelia Korf in Blackfoot, Idaho, in 1897 and had six children.

Generation	Period	Family Tree
24	1897-1989	Earl Jennings Nyhart.
	1898-1997	Orrie Emmel Nyhart.
	1901-1967	Thomas Lester Nyhart
	1902-1996	Opal Fern Nyhart Cox.
	1906	Infant boy died at birth and unnamed.
	1910-1994	Maynard Arthur Nyhart.

Frances Korf & Jordan "Jerd" Nyhart
Wedding, 1897

Jerd & Frances Nyhart, 1925

Earl & Orrie Nyhart, 1899

*Jordan "Jerd," Maynard, Frances,
Orrie, Earl, Lester & Opal Nyhart, ca. 1916*

*Orrie, Earl, Opal & Lester Nyhart,
ca. 1905*

Maynard, Orrie, Jerd, Earl,
Frances & Lester, 1936

Generation	Family Tree
24	There were six children of "Jerd" and Frances Nyhart:
	Earl Jennings Nyhart. Earl's first wife was Julia Barnosky, and they had two children. His second wife was Doris Rosamond Eder, and they had one child.
	Orrie Emmel Nyhart. He married Mae Cocanougher and had two children.
	Thomas Lester Nyhart. He remained unmarried.
	Opal Fern Nyhart Cox. She married C.J. Cox, and they had four children.
	A son died in infancy, and they refused to name him.
	Maynard Arthur Nyhart. He married Thelma Ellen Anderson, and they had two children.
25	There were eleven grandchildren of "Jerd" and Frances Nyhart:
	Leland Baker Nyhart, Willis Harold Nyhart, Elsie Evelyn Nyhart, Sharon Marie Nyhart, Jerald "Buzz" Lee Nyhart, Frances Belle Cox, Donald Eugene Cox, Lillian Mae Cox, Virginia Gayle Cox, Therlean Joy Nyhart, and Lela May Nyhart.

Generation	Family Tree
26	There were 33 great-grandchildren of Jerd and Frances Nyhart:

Kathy Nyhart, William C.T. Nyhart, Nancy Beth Nyhart Lampe, Leland Nyhart, Victoria Nyhart, Earl Jordan Dodd, Petra Lee Dodd, Heidi Smith Woods, Chad O. E. Smith, Brian Jordan Smith, Jon L. Nyhart, Justin Nyhart, Jeffrey D. Holland, Fred Holland, Rex Holland, Patsy L. Cox Selway, Donna Jean Cox Davis, Thomas Don Cox, Carson Jay Cox, Layne Earl Carlson, Lloyd Carlson, Lyle Carlson, Terry Gayle Beck Novich, Linda Lee Beck Romandelli, Ronald Rex Beck, Jody Fern Beck Olmstead, Henry Maynard Merrick, Melanie Merrick Keyser, Mitchell Merrick, Jimilea VanMeter Grose, Blaine VanMeter, Duana L. VanMeter Van Buren, and Chaini R. VanMeter Bronec. |

Generation	Family Tree
27	Great-grandchildren of Earl Nyhart: Heidi LuAnne Nyhart, William Troy Nyhart, Michael Buckingham, Robert Buckingham, Melissa Buckingham. Heather Buckingham, Christopher Nyhart, David Nyhart, Rachael Nyhart, Jordan Dodd, Brandon Dodd, and Daniel Rodriguez. Great-grandchildren of Orrie Nyhart: Dean Smith, Taylor Smith, Evan Smith, Adisyn Nyhart, Kassidi Nyhart, Averie Nyhart, Reighly Nyhart, Dristin Nyhart, Quinten Nyhart, and Colton Nyhart. Great-grandchildren of Opal Nyhart Cox: Melissa Holland, Brock Holland, Kelsey Holland, Alyssa Holland, Michael Selway, Shannon Selway, Debbie Davis, Tracy Davis, Bruce Cox (deceased), Leah Cox, Clinton Cox, Casey Cox, Kimberly Cox, Tanner Cox, Britney Cox, Erin Carlson, Kelly Carlson, Lance Carlson, Scott Novich, Chris Novich, Jeni Romandelli, Shan Romaandelli, Allison Beck, Tanner Siderius, and Scott Martin. Great-grandchildren of Maynard Nyhart: Alyta Merrick, Morgan Merrick, Randon VanMeter, Krystl Grose Kulbeck, William (Dude) Grose, Suzan Grose Lehman, and Tara VanMeter.

Coming to America

The 18th generation Johan George, Sr. was born in Rumbach, Germany, on the 29th of January 1716. He had a twin sister, Susanna Maria, that never left Rumbach. His younger sister, Anna Elizabeth, was born on the 4th of February 1718. She immigrated to America later and married Johann Conradt Weinmuller. In early 1737, at 21 years old, George, Sr., his half-brother Friedrich,38, and his wife and children, his cousin Michael, 24, and his wife and children and his 15-year-old cousin Jacob received permission from the German state of Rhineland-Palatinate (Pfalz) to go to the "new land."

They traveled on the Rhine River to Rotterdam while crossing 20 custom checkpoints en route down the river. After a few weeks in Rotterdam, they booked ship passage on St. Andrew. They arrived in Philadelphia on the 26th of September 1737. They marched immediately to the courthouse and subscribed Oaths to King George of England and the provincial government.

St. Andrew, 1737,
The Neiharts at sea

Ship Harbor,
Rotterdam, Netherlands, 1737,
The Neiharts departure

They traveled to the Pennsylvania frontier in Bucks County, close to the town of Egypt. They took up lands to farm there, mainly in the Heidelberg township. In 1743, George Sr. married Anna Catherine Sensinger. They raised nine children. George and Anna are buried near Schoenersville, Pennsylvania.

Their oldest, George Jr., was the first of our family to be born in America. He was born in 1749 near present-day Emerald, Pennsylvania. George Jr. married Maria Magdalena Sterner in 1768. They lived on his in-laws' farms. He was a blacksmith by trade but also farmed. During the American Revolution, he was enrolled in his local militia company under Capt. John Santee. George, Jr. was first a corporal, then a Sergeant. He then performed several tours as a Lieutenant in the Continental Service. George, Jr. and Maria Magdalena raised six children: George Henry, John, George, Magdalena, Julia, and Daniel.

The 20th generation was John Neuhart. He was born on 15 June 1774 and married Maria Magdalena Henry raising 12 children: Salome, Sarah, George, Maria, Anna, Juliana, William, Adam, Elizabeth, Jacob, Joseph, and Reuben.

The 21st generation was Adam Nihart, born on the 4th of March 1805, in Luzerne, Pennsylvania. He died on the 4th of December 1902 and is buried at the Old Stone Cemetery near Dodgeville, Iowa. Adam and his first wife, Susanna, had nine children: Silas, John, Washington, Phineas, Mary, Sylvester, Joseph, Sally Ann, and Julia. Adam and his second wife, Catherine Smith, had one son Andrew. Adam's third wife, Ann Parmer, had no children, and it ended quickly in a divorce.

Adam and Susanna lived in Luzerne until her death on the 10th of February 1854. She is buried in the Newport Cemetery in Luzerne, Pennsylvania.

Adam became a large landowner, but after his wife's death, he started selling off parcels of land. In the fall of 1856, he married his second wife, Catherine. In 1857 they moved to Iowa. There he lived the rest of his life. He is buried in the Old Stone Cemetery near Dodgeville, Iowa, with his third son.

George Washington Nihart is the 22nd generation of Nyharts and the author's great grandfather. It was about this time that they changed the surname spelling to Nyhart. George Washington was always called 'Wash.'

Traveling West to the Montana Territory

Wash Nyhart was born and schooled in Luzerne, Pennsylvania, on the 13th of August 1836. He lived there until he was 21 years old. Then, he accompanied his father Adam, his stepmother and his eight siblings to Franklin Township, Iowa. When he was 25 years old, he journeyed to Greene County, Illinois. He married his cousin Mary Linder on the 24th of September 1861. In 1862, Franklin County, Iowa, enrolled men to be drafted for the Civil War. Brothers Levi, Phineas, and Wash were among the men enrolled. Wash avoided being called up by signing on to the wagon train heading west. According to law then, one was exempt when living in a territory. The family used to tease Wash about avoiding the draft. Levi and Phineas were drafted and fought in the Civil War.

Wagon Train, 1864

On the 17th of April 1864, Wash Nyhart, his wife Mary, their two sons George junior, two years old and Jordan, five months old, joined Mary's parents, George and Mary senior. On the journey, Linder, Mary junior's brother Jasper, his wife Catherine, their two children Cordelia, age four, and Hattie, age two. Mary senior's nephew James Linder, his wife Virginia, and their 1-year-old daughter Florence. The group headed west with family, several friends, and neighbor boys. Oxen pulled the Nyhart and Linder wagons. One of the original ox yokes is displayed in the Museum in Twin Bridges, Montana.

Ox Yoke, ca. 1864

Wagon Train West with Oxen, ca. 1864

They journeyed from Dodgeville, Iowa, to Council Bluffs, Iowa, where they met with other wagons heading west. The wagon train was headed for the goldfields in the Territory of Idaho. The Virginia City, Montana area was in the Washington Territory until 1862. Then this region became the Territory of Idaho in 1863. On the 26th of May 1864, the Montana Territory was carved out of the Idaho Territory and present-day Wyoming was transferred to the Dakota Territory. The wagon train was near Fort Kearny, Nebraska, when President Abraham Lincoln made Bannack and Virginia City part of the Montana Territory. After crossing the Missouri River to Omaha, they traveled along the Platte River.

Wagon Train River Crossing, ca. 1864

They met with the wagon train at Richard's Bridge (now approximately Casper, Wyoming). A.A. Townsend led the Townsend wagon train as the captain. The guides were John Baptiste Boyer and Rafael Gallegos. The wagon master was Van Sickels. They left Richard's Bridge on the 28th of June and traveled the Bozeman Trail.

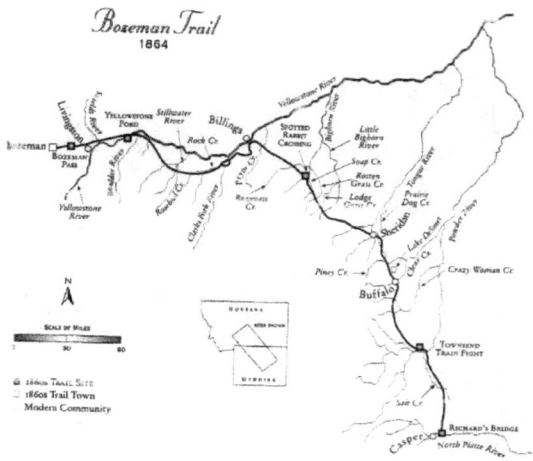

Bozeman Trail, 1864

On the 7th of July 1864, at their Powder River campsite, they became surrounded by Indians. The Nyhart and Linder wagons had ten men, four women, and five children. Jasper Linder's wife was pregnant then, and she gave birth shortly after arriving in Alder Gulch, Montana Territory. The Nyhart and Linder group possessed about 20 Henry repeating 16-shot 44 caliber rimfire breech-loading rifles and ten shotguns. Amongst them, they also had several six-shooters. They were well-armed to defend themselves for the journey. Many wagon men had other weapons, including Henrys, Spencers, squirrel rifles (22's), shotguns, and Colt revolvers.

Spotted Cow led the Powder River Indian raid. Three tribes of Northern Cheyenne, Oglala, and Sioux were involved in this fight. According to Wash and other members, the fight lasted six hours. Wash's diary of the trip west is in the

Montana Historical Society Archives in Helena, Montana. It was recorded that Townsend and his crew could "shoot 1700 times" without reloading. When the fighting ended, only four men and about a dozen Indians' lives were lost in the attack.

The extended, overland journey west required many supplies and included the following provisions. Each family of four was to have on their wagon for the trip west ten pounds rice, 200 pounds flour, 75 pounds bacon, five pounds coffee, two pounds tea, 25 pounds sugar, a small keg of molasses, half a bushel dried beans, one bushel dried fruit, two pounds saleratus (baking soda), ten pounds salt, half a bushel cornmeal, a small keg of vinegar, ten pounds jerky, five gallons whiskey (mainly for medicinal purposes?), three gallons wine, and 25 pounds of soap.

Other requirements were two pairs of shoes for each person, cast-iron dutch ovens, skillets, pots, pans, eating utensils, a coffee grinder, and a first aid kit. The wagon's supply and equipment included knives, saws, shovels, axes, hammers, grinding stones, a washboard, tubs, and barrels for water and food. Of course, bedding and clothing were also needed. The women stored their breakable dishes in the flour barrels, for example. No space went to waste. The supply list was substantial since four families were in the wagon train. They also brought tools, anvil, ropes, whips, extra shoes for the oxen, and replacement rims for the wagon wheels.

At the start of the journey, the Townsend wagon train consisted of 150 wagons, 375 men, 36 women, and 56 children under 16. There were 636 oxen, 194 cows, ten mules, and 79 horses. Our group had four covered wagons and four supply wagons. Each wagon required four to six oxen and many extras when needed (e.g., crossing a river or muddy area).

Homesteading in Montana

On 20 September 1864, they arrived in Virginia City and Nevada City of the Montana Territory. Immediately upon arrival, the men erected log cabins. Shortly after, Wash came down with Rocky Mountain tick fever. He suffered a long recovery. Wash worked as a miner for one year and six months as a teamster. He decided to leave the mines and raise horses and cattle. He declared that more money was earned in selling horses and beef to the miners and new settlers than in mining. He took up land by the Point of Rocks in the Beaverhead Valley. His brother-in-law Jasper Linder left the mining profession and adjoined Wash's land as a rancher and farmer. This land settlement started the extensive Nyhart and Linder Ranches.

The mines with their miners and settlers needed riding and working horses, which drove the ranches to run a thousand horses' heads. These families kept busy breaking saddle horses and plow horses. In their spare time, the children learned to ride bareback early. Eventually, the families ventured into sheep farming and cattle ranching.

Original Linder Log Home, present-day

Wash and Mary were the parents of George Washington Jr., Jordan Luccins, Columbus Albert, John Adam, Mary Delila, Susan Emeline, Charles Edward, Ernest Gilbert, William Sylvester, Thomas Leander, and Eliza Amelia, a total of 11 children.

*George "Wash" Nyhart in front of
first log barn, ca. 1869*

All but the first two were all born at home. All the children took an active part in the operation. Jasper and Catherine Linder had six children: Cordelia Catherine, Hattie Nevada, Luella Florence, Anthony Vernon, William Wesley, and Austin Arthur.

Besides raising horses, the Nyhart and Linder duo raised cattle, pigs, and sheep. With nearly 3000 head of cattle, they advertised and sold their beef as "Treasure Steaks" on the hoof. Shearing time with approximately 5000 head of sheep was a massive operation. It took several weeks to accomplish the work as it was all done by hand.

Austin A. Linder Shearing Crew, ca. 1920

FROM

Sheep Shearers' Merchandise
and Commission Co.

BOX 1902   BUTTE, MONT.

TO

A. A. LINDER,
% MOTOR INN,
TWIN BRIDGES, MONT.

Contents-Merchandise Fourth Class Mail

Post Master: This package may be opened for postal inspection if necessary. If not delivered in 15 days return to us.

WE GUARANTEE RETURN POSTAGE.

*Shipping Label for
Shearing Equipment, ca. 1920*

Wash built a sizable one-room log cabin with substantial hewn logs, and then he put down a wood slab floor. Having placed small logs very close together for the roof, he covered the roof with dirt and packed sod firmly down on top of the dirt. From there, he raised his large family.

One-room Log Cabin, ca. 1908

The Shoshone Indians always camped close on their annual fishing and hunting trips. They were a friendly tribe and loved Mary's cooking, especially her home-baked bread. The Shoshones always brought deerskin gloves for the men that the Indian squaws had made. In mid-1878, the Nez Perce Indians were on their flight. Many men joined the Federal Troops to defend their homes. The Horse Prairie Raid and the Battle of the Big Hole were about to materialize. The Nyhart and Linder clan prepared for a possible attack, not knowing what route the Nez Perce would take. The attack happened far west of them.

Nevertheless, they took shelter on the Beaverhead River in the thick willows and brush as the Nez Perce made their way west. The family went to Birch Creek for their winter wood as the valley only had willows and brush and no trees, thus offering no protection from the Montana winters. The Shoshone Indians continually let them go through as the Nyhart and Linder families gave them meat to make pemmican.

Some of the settlers in the valley never treated the Indians kindly, so they never got the privilege for wood gathering as the Indians controlled the Birch Creek area. Wash had an incredibly sophisticated whiskey still up Trout Creek. They had an elite bunch of businesses in Butte City buying their moonshine. Thankfully, they were never caught by the "lawmen." Some men went to the Rochester Basin to do their moonshining. They put their stills underground. In winter, one could see the smoke rising from holes in the ground. One wonders how they escaped getting caught.

When the family started farming, they needed more and more water to irrigate the fields. Wash diverted the water from the Beaverhead River around the Point of Rocks.

POINT 'O' ROCK - SOUTH TWIN BRIDGES, MONT.

Point of Rocks, ca. 1870

Unfortunately, he blew off the Lewis and Clark inscription they carved in the rocks, not knowing it would be part of history. Lewis and Clark had camped on land that the Nyhart and Linder families acquired. Sacagawea, a Lemhi Shoshone woman guide, traveled with the Lewis and Clark Expedition in 1805 and recognized this rock formation and knew that she might be in the vicinity of her relatives.

Wash's son Jordan became active in operation and took over as the older generation slowed down. Jordan was called Jerd by the family. Jerd is our 23rd generation in the Nyhart family tree, and he married his cousin, Frances Amelia Korf, from Mediapolis, Iowa. They were married on the 2nd of February 1897. Frances traveled from Iowa to Blackfoot, Idaho, by train, where Jerd met her, and they were married there. The couple returned and settled a few miles north of his father, Wash. Frances and Jerd raised six children: Earl Jennings (my father), Orrie Emmel, Thomas Lester, Opal Fern, a baby dying in infancy, and Maynard Arthur, which became our 24th generation. In 1897, a big red barn replaced the old log barn. Frances was pregnant with her firstborn and sat whittling all the wood pegs needed to put the rafters and beams together. The barn is still being used by the family today.

Spring 1899, the word was received that a traveling preacher would be in the area. Jerd and Frances spread the word that church services would be held at their ranch. People came from around the valley and enjoyed the preaching of Brother Van Orsdal. They enjoyed a potluck dinner afterward. After the dinner, Brother Van Orsdal, a traveling Methodist Circuit Preacher, baptized Orrie, six months old and Earl, at 20-months.

Jerd put a thick layer of sand on the roof of the family ranch's rock milk house. He covered it with a fine screen. Frances would put her thinly sliced fruits, vegetables, and herbs that she grew on the roof. Then it was covered with more screens and secured so the bugs and flies could not enter. This contraption was Frances's solar dehydrator. During this period, everybody had sturdy log homes. However, in 1903, brothers William and Austin Linder decided to order a prefab home. They ordered one out of the Sears and Roebuck catalog for $1500—an expensive purchase in those days. The home model that Sadie picked was "The Seven Gables."

Linder Seven Gable Ranch House,
ca. 1950

It was shipped by rail to Dillon, Montana and brought to the ranch by wagons. The new home was modern with a gravity-flow, ceiling-tank toilet and a clawfoot cast iron tub adorning the bathroom. For electricity, they installed a

Delco system. In later years, everybody in the valley was connected to a rural electric system called the REA (now the Vigilante Electric Cooperative). The Delco building was later used as a fuel house.

In 1909, Jerd and son Earl were falling cottonwood trees over the hills on the Joe Ziegler place along the Big Hole River. One tree twisted when falling and was heading towards Earl, so Jerd pushed Earl out of the way of the tree. In doing so, it caught Jerd's ankle and crushed it badly; Jerd also broke his arm. Orrie, then age 11, was sent for Dr. Baker and Dr. Bond. Frances kept giving Jerd whiskey to dull the pain. After Orrie and the doctors arrived, Frances held the lantern. The doctors laid Jerd on the kitchen table while Earl and Orrie held their father down while the doctors sawed Jerd's foot off with the kitchen meat saw.

After his leg healed, Earl, 12 by then, took Jerd to Dillon, Montana in the wagon. They boarded the train for Salt Lake City, where he was fitted with a wooden foot strapped to his leg that fit perfectly to his shoe. With the fitting complete, they returned to Dillon, got their team and wagon from the livery stable, and headed home.

Oh, how the author loved to beg her grandfather to take his foot off and then watch him put it back on—what a sight for a child.

Because of Jerd's condition with his foot, at ages 12 and 11, Earl and Orrie were given the job of operating the ranch. Lester and Opal helped with the small chores, like feeding the chickens and caring for their father. The following year, baby brother Maynard was welcomed into the family.

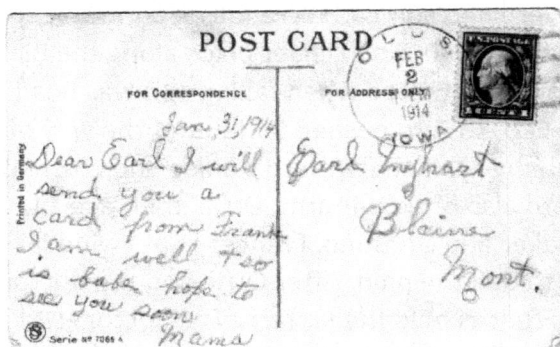

Frances Nyhart Post Card to
Son Earl, 1914

Throughout the year, the women raised their chickens and turkeys. The young turkeys were fried like chickens—it was one of my father's favorite dishes. Some of the larger turkeys were sold, and the rest were saved for the families to eat. The women brooded their chickens. So, there were always lots of young roosters to eat. The pullets were saved for egg-laying. There was always a 'broody hen,' so they always had a fresh supply of baby chicks.

The five Nyhart Ranches each had two pairs of work-horses. Earl Jennings named his Nig and Chub and the other Dick and Dyke. Each ranch owned several saddle horses. They used them for working the cattle and sheep. The saddle horses were also used to carry the canvas dams along the ditches during flood irrigation. For haying, they used overshot derricks to stack the loose-cut hay.

Earl Nyhart Ranch, ca. 1960

Orrie Nyhart Ranch, ca. 1960

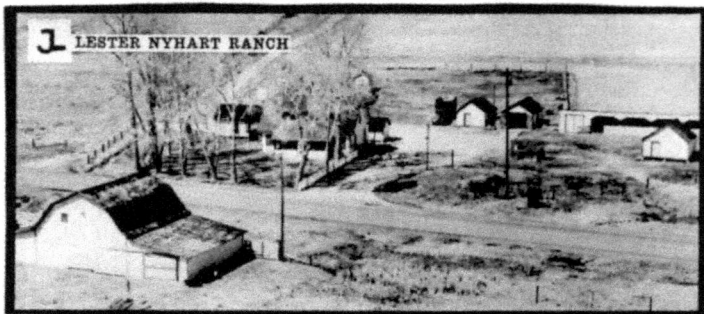

Lester Nyhart Ranch, ca. 1960

C. J. Cox & Opal Nyhart Ranch, ca. 1960

Maynard Nyhart Ranch, ca. 1960

Jerd's brother, John Nyhart, left the ranch and moved to north Dillon, Montana. He started a Nyhart Silver Fox Farm and had many silver foxes. Fox fur was trendy back then, being used as trim on coat collars. I remember mother's fox fur-trimmed coat as John cured and sold the fur to various furriers in New York City. He would buy old canner horses to feed the foxes, and the local boys would bring the carp and suckers they caught to John to feed the foxes. When the depression hit, there was no demand for fur, so he released the foxes into the wild.

41

Silver Fox on Nyhart Fox Farm,
ca. 1930

The valley had a telephone party line back in the 30s, 40s and 50s. There were 12 on the party line. One had to crank a handle on the side of the phone to get the operator to answer. Two women in Twin Bridges worked as the local operators. The operator would ask whom you wanted her to talk to. She would punch in the number, and it would ring in all 12 phones. My parents' number was 15J1, and it was one long ring. There were 12 different rings, from one short or one long to several different combinations of short and long rings such as one short and two long or one long and one short, etc.

Everybody knew who was being called. You could listen in to any of the calls. It was the fastest gossip spreader of that era. In 1949, the valley got phones with the dial-up system and new telephone numbers, but still on a party line. Then around 1960, long-distance calls could be made.

The road from the Point of Rocks to Twin Bridges was a narrow dirt road, with a little gravel mixed in.

Early Bridge Crossing the Beaverhead River
by the Point of Rocks, ca. 1890

The Nyhart and Linder area was tree lined. In the spring when the thaw began, the road was filled with frost boils. Few people traveled this road. Most people turned at the Point of Rocks and took the graveled road on the east side of the Beaverhead River to get to Twin Bridges or Sheridan.

Second Bridge Crossing, ca. 1930

The school bus and mailman were the only daily travelers. The kids always piled to the back of the bus, putting more weight there so it would get stuck. It was a great excuse to be late for school. The mailman always used great caution maneuvering his old pickup on the dirt road. The school bus driver and mailman were the happiest to see the road paved. In the winter, the road was almost impassable with large snowdrifts. It was a fun place for the kids to play.

The road was covered with water that drained from the irrigated fields in the spring and summer. Finally, in 1951, the highway department took all the trees out (imminent domain overruled the landowners), widened and built up the road. They started paving sections from the cut at the Point of Rocks for several miles. It took a few years to finish the paving to Twin Bridges.

Summer and Fall Activities

Horses were used to mow and rake the hay. Horse-driven buck rakes (or hay sweeps) were used to push the hay windrows to the stackers. Not long after, they used power buck rakes to push the hay to the derricks. The hired help would sprinkle rock salt on the loose hay in the stacks every few loads of hay. That kept the hay from spoiling and benefited the livestock when fed to them in the winter and spring. Next was the chore of fencing around each haystack. They used posts, barbed wire, and pole panels to make hay corrals. Until 1951, the Nyharts used workhorses until they bought tractors.

Bringing in the wild horses in the fall was a big and dangerous job. Several different rodeo producers would come and watch the cowboys buck out the broncs. They sold lots of horses to the rodeo and even had several in the National Finals. The fall was also stud colt cutting time. Ralph Redfield was the "go-to" man for that job. Nobody could surpass Ralph at cutting colts or horseshoeing. During World War I, Ralph was in the cavalry and horseshoed up to 100 ponies per day.

The Nyhart and Linder women spent many long hours in the summer and fall canning and preserving their garden produce. They would put up several hundred jars of vegetables, fruit, meats, pickles and relishes, jams, and jellies. That made for many a tasty meal in the cold winter months to come.

In the fall, when the apples ripened, the family would load up a wagon with barrels and jugs and headed to the Davis Ranch (now the White Rock Ranch) in Waterloo, Montana, where a large apple orchard grew. Apples were pressed into cider. The women came home and heated the apple juice and canned it; otherwise, it would turn into vinegar.

The men dreaded hunting season as the deer and elk would mingle with their livestock. It only took one careless (or desperate) hunter to kill a calf or start a stampede. The families ate little wild game because they could butcher their beef and hogs.

As the men worked with the herds in the fall, the women spent time working with their flocks of chickens, turkeys, and geese. They kept their eyes peeled for the birds that did not lay eggs. Those barren hens and dames were slaughtered and canned for later use (e.g., homemade noodles). The pullets were laying eggs by the late fall, and the flocks were replenished every year.

Coffee substitutes were used when times were lean. Coffee was a luxury and costly. After popcorn was popped, the "old maids" (unpopped kernels) were saved in a tin pan at the back of the wood cookstove where the kernels would roast and darken. When the kernels are ready, the women grind them for a coffee brew. The exact process was used with barley kernels. The children loved the substitute coffee, especially with fresh-milked cream and honey. Sometimes the women would mix real coffee with these substitutes to give the brew a recognizable coffee flavor. Nothing was left to waste in lean times.

Spring and Summer Activities

Grandmother (Frances) loved looking for honeybees down in the cottonwood groves along the Beaverhead River. She would sit on a log and watch which tree the bees continually entered. That "honey tree" got a big red ribbon tied around it. Then during the coldest part of winter, they would cut the tree down and retrieve the honey. They always had a supply for baking and eating. Frances's garden was one to behold. She planted many vegetables. One never touched the last two feet of any vegetable row she planted during harvesting. That area was left to go to seed for next year's crop. She would put paper sacks over the ripening seeds and tie the sacks. She seldom had to purchase any seeds for planting.

Berries were numerous; there were many gooseberries, currants, and chokecherries in the valley. The women and children would pick the berries, and the men would take them by wagon to Butte City. They sold their berries to the miners and businesses and used the proceeds to buy shearing supplies, horseshoes, cloth, sewing supplies, and whatever was needed. This business trek was a three-day trip to Butte City, going over the Cedar Hills and finally down Roosevelt Drive. They camped out for two nights.

Not to be overlooked, the Nyhart men loved their pheasants. In the spring, before flood irrigation began, the men would walk the ditches looking for nests. They would build them up on dirt mounds so the floodwater could not reach the birds and ruin the nests. They did the same procedure for duck and geese nests. This protection helped keep the bird population from declining. The Nyharts were conservationists at heart and loved the land.

Calving season was a massive operation each spring, with several brandings at each ranch using their brands. Cattle drives in the spring to the summer ranges were a significant endeavor—as were the fall roundups. Many horses and cowboys were needed and a camp tender and cook.

When the Beaverhead River water level was low in late summer, they dug for river clams. When they got a washtub full, a feast was had. After the Clarks Canyon Dam was built, that ended the clam digging.

There was a big apple tree by the Point of Rocks Cemetery. When Decoration Day came, it was time to decorate the graves. The women and girls would collect wild iris blossoms and yellow bee flower blossoms and add them to the apple blossoms from the apple tree. Moreover, if the lilacs were in bloom, they were added to the jars and tin cans the women saved. There were no store-bought wreaths or flowers at that time.

When there was a break in the summer months, the men and boys would head to the timber to cut poles. The small diameter poles were used to make pole panels to fence the haystacks, with the larger poles were used for corrals. The young boys were relegated to making the panels. Then the boys were rewarded with a swim in the river.

Shooting gophers in the summer was an excellent sport for the kids. It also sharpened their hunting skills. Both boys and girls were taught gun safety and to be able to defend themselves.

Winter Activities

There were many rattlesnakes in the hills west of the main ranch house. The men would have rattlesnake hunts. On the coldest winter day, they would look for steam coming from under the rocky ledges. Using a shepherd's hook, they pulled out a single snake, then a stick of dynamite was attached with a long fuse. The snake was pushed back in its den but not before the fuse was lit. It usually killed a dozen or more snakes using that method.

There were holes drilled in the floor for drainage. The icehouse held the stores of canned and dried goods throughout the year. During the winter, the men used ice saws and cut ice blocks in the river. The blocks were packed with lots of sawdust and stored in the icehouse. No sawdust ever went to waste. After electricity came to the valley, refrigerators and freezers replaced the block ice operation. There was an icehouse on the home Nyhart place. It was built with thick walls and a floor.

After being decommissioned, the icehouse became a playhouse for the children. Each ranch had two or more milk cows. There was always plenty of milk for everybody, especially the barn cats. The cream was churned into butter. The leftover buttermilk never went to waste. Everybody owned hand-crank ice cream freezers, so we all enjoyed ice cream regularly. Puddings and custards were made with extra milk and cream. The leftover milk and table scraps were fed to the pigs. Nothing went to waste.

In the wintertime, the men and boys went ice fishing. They would bring the fish they caught and soaked them in a brown sugar and salt solution. Then the fish were dried and smoked. The men and boys did many trappings in the winter when the fur was prime. They trapped a lot of muskrats, beavers, otters, and mink.

When cured and stretched, the fur pelts brought in extra cash when sold to a fur dealer. They hunted ducks and geese. The women saved all the down for making pillows. Moreover, they ate the meat. Even a stray squab (pigeon) made it to the dinner table.

A Quick Excursion with A.J. Nyhart

Drama and courtroom gymnastics, not quite Perry Mason style, was exhibited in September 1894. The author's great-great-grandfather, Adam J. Nyhart, the recent harvest of oats and wheat valued at $350, burned bright and hot. Nothing was left. A.J. "knew" whom to blame and where a set of footprints at the crime scene led—his neighbor Samuel Plunkett. A trial was called, and the day was hot. The courtroom was packed, full of witnesses and those looking for something exciting. Witness after witness was called, and the prosecution's star witness finally stepped on the stand. E.E. Coolbaugh, it seemed, had stepped out of the courtroom to imbibe in a few beers and whiskeys (he could not remember how many beers while under oath when questioned). Mr. Coolbaugh could not remember much, and he was allowed to step down. The judge, being hot and hungry as it was lunchtime, and with the courtroom crowd now cheering Mr. Coolbaugh as he walked out to the nearest bar, ruled that Mr. Plunkentt was innocent. Everyone, including A.J., scattered for lunch.

Nyhart German Heritage Never Forgotten

The family was always considered a German Clan. They shared much of the workload and always were available to help each other. Seven pigs were butchered at a time. What a chore, for the women had to scrape the bristly hair from the scalded carcasses. Then came the trimming off the fat and rendering it. The melted lard was put in tin pails with tight-fitting lids. Nothing was wasted on the pig—not even the squeal as I used to hear. Another delicacy made by the women was headcheese, souse, and pickled pigs' feet and ears. They washed the intestines repeatedly to fill them with spicy sausage meat made ready to be smoked. The bacon, jowl meat, and hams were all smoked. Can you smell it? The home Linder ranch had an extensive communal cellar and smokehouse.

And let us not forget the kraut. Big crocks of sauerkraut were fermented each fall. Furthermore, jerky was made along with crocks of cured corned beef when the beef was butchered. Some of the meat was canned or frozen, the rest eaten fresh.

The Later Generations Summarized

The following information is about relatives to George Washington (Wash) Nyhart. Wash was married to Mary Elizabeth Linder on 24th September 1861.

Their children were:

- George Washington, Jr. 1862-1935. His wife was Kate Shewmaker.
- Jordan Luccins (Jerd) 1863-1945. His wife was Frances Amelia Korf.
- Columbus Albert 1866-1947. His wife was Della Putnam.
- John Adam 1868-1943. His wife was Clarinda Vada Engle.
- Mary Delila 1870-1910. Her husband was William (Webb) Stewart.
- Susan Emeline 1872-1872. She died shortly after birth.
- Charles Edward 1873-1943. He was never married.
- Ernest Gilbert 1876-1958. His wife was Eliza Frances Estell Day.
- William Sylvester 1878-1916. His wife was Susie Leta Stalcup.
- Thomas Leander 1880-1901. He was never married.
- Eliza Amelia 1882-1890. Eliza died of influenza at eight.

George Washington Linder was born in Tennessee in 1804. He passed away in 1881 and is buried in the Point of Rocks Cemetery. He married his cousin Mary Linder in1833. Mary was born in Tennessee in 1802, passed away in 1889, and is also buried in the Point of Rocks Cemetery. He was 60 years old, and Mary was 62 when they joined the wagon train in 1864 to travel the Bozeman Trail to Montana.

They had the following children.

- Nancy Jane 1833-1902. Husband was Cary Shelledy. They had nine children.
- Dicey Emeline 1835-1896. Her husband was Hiriam Fleenor. They had 11 children.
- William Jasper 1836-1906. He married Catherine Bayles. They had six children.
- Mary Elizabeth 1838-1903. She married Wash Nyhart. They had 11 children.
- Sidney 1841-1927. Spouse unknown.
- Lydia 1842-unknown. Spouse unknown.

George Washington Linder's parents were Jacob Linder and Dicey Wood Linder. Mary Linder's parents were Joseph Jefferson Linder and Nancy Christian Linder.

William Jasper Linder was nicknamed Jap. He was born in Tennessee in 1836. He passed away in 1906 and is buried in the Point of Rocks Cemetery. His wife Catherine was born in Ohio, passed away on the home ranch in 1887 and was buried in the Point of Rocks Cemetery. Catherine's parents were Joseph Bayles and Lucy Wallace.

They had the following children:

- Cordelia Catherine 1860-1883. Her husband was Leander Goetchius, and they had Edna.
- Hattie Nevada 1862-1928. Her husband was Charles Green with no children.
- Luella Florence 184-1946. Her husband was Chris A. Dillet. They had four children.

- Anthony Vernon 1868-1920. His first wife was Emma Jane Wilson with no children. His second wife was Inez Goetschius, and they had Georgia and Harley.
- William Wesley 1872-1903. He married his cousin Sarah (Sadie) Elizabeth Fleenor with no children.
- Austin Arthur 1876-1941. After his brother died, he married Sadie. They had a son Clyde that died in infancy.

When visiting the Point of Rocks Cemetery south of Twin Bridges, Montana, one will find many of the names on these pages. Several Nyhart descendants live on and work the original Nyhart and Linder homesteads, making the family tree's 26th and 27th generations.

Point of Rocks Cemetery, present-day

Family Notoriety

Famous people in our family tree are Allen Neuharth, president of Gannett Newspaper Corporation, owning 83 daily newspapers. Comedian and actor Bob Newhart; and Russell Schweickart, an astronaut on Apollo IX who walked in space for 45 minutes. John Gneisenau Neihardt was an author and poet of over 30 books about the Lakota Plains Indians. Another famous family member was James Leroy Neihart, the founder and first mayor of Neihart, Montana. He was a cousin of Wash.

More Family Portraits

Earl Nyhart, 1932

Willis & Leland Nyhart, 1928

Earl, Doris & Evelyn, 1943

Evelyn & Doris Nyhart, 1944

Earl & Doris Nyhart, 1960

Orrie, Mae & Sherry Nyhart, 1944

Sherry Nyhart, 1947

Jerry "Buzz" Nyhart, 1949

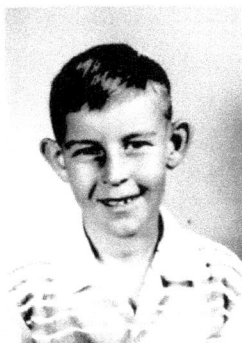

Jerry "Buzz" Nyhart, ca. 1954

Sherry & Evelyn Nyhart, 1946

Lester Nyhart, 1950

Opal Nyhart, 1919

Jeff & Opal Cox Wedding, 1921

Cox's Family, 1937

Frances Belle Cox, 1935

Don Cox, ca. 1932

Lillian Cox, 1947

Virginia Gayle Cox, 1943

Maynard Nyhart
High School
Graduation, 1930

Maynard & Thelma Nyhart, 1932

Maynard, Thelma & Therlean Nyhart, 1943

Therlean Nyhart, 1937

Lela May Nyhart, 1945

Therlean, Lela May, Jerry "Buzz,"
Sherry & Evelyn Nyhart, 2008

Maynard & Thelma Nyhart's 50th Anniversary
Doris, Earl, Maynard, Thelma, Opal,
Mae & Orrie Nyhart, 1981

Linder Death Notice, 1897/1906

Linder Coat of Arms

Acknowledgment

The Nyhart family tree and history was reviewed, supplemented, and corrected where necessary by Dr. Dennis Kastens. His support and encouragement are appreciated. Additional thanks go to Earl J. Dodd for helping with the review and publication support.

About the Author

Elsie Evelyn Nyhart Dodd is the daughter of the eldest in Generation 24. Evelyn was born in the parsonage of the Christ Episcopal Church in Sheridan, Montana. She spent the first 24 years living on the Linder home ranch that her father had purchased from the Linder Estate. Evelyn's father was the family's storyteller and kept meticulous records for generations to enjoy. Evelyn has enjoyed genealogy for over 30 years. She has published the *Nyhart Family Cookbook* that captures country tastes.

Evelyn Nyhart Dodd, 2022

www.ingramcontent.com/pod-product-compliance
Lightning Source LLC
Chambersburg PA
CBHW070029030426
42335CB00017B/2353